The Magic of Chelsea

NOTEBOOK

A Flower Show
Like No Other

Christine Thompson-Wells

Copyright© 2023 MSI Australia

All rights reserved.

ISBN: 978-1-7636806-2-3

Published by How2Books
Under license from MSI Ltd, Australia
Company Registration No: 96963518255
NSW, Australia

See our website: www.how2books.com.au
Or contact by email: sales@how2books.com.au
Covers and Copyright owned by MSI, Australia

MSI acknowledges the author and images, text and photographs used in this book.

Published by How2Books

10% of each book's sale helps support Diabetes Type One and Cancer Research.

Swaddle Baby Orchid

Your Notes

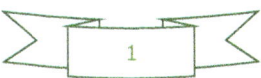

8

Friendships At Chelsea – Chelsea Pensioners

Traditional Flowers in Amazing

Displays...

24

Traditional Semi-Curve Floral Arrangement – Elegant in Line & Construction...

Masses of Colour...

Could You Ask for More...!

www.ingramcontent.com/pod-product-compliance
Lightning Source LLC
Chambersburg PA
CBHW061741070526
44585CB00024B/2770